DAMIAN C. AMAZU

ART. DAN A. BARONGO

PEACE IS AWESOME.

By Damian Chukwurah Amazu

Art by Dan Abohawenka Barongo

I dedicate this book to world peace and all the wonderful, peaceful, intelligent, brave, courageous, and determined children who want to be literate in life. Also, to all the great children who respect their parents, and are willing to achieve greater goals in the future.

I respect and acknowledge all my readers and wish you tremendous success in life.

I will discuss peace in fifteen categories as illustrated in this book to improve personal peace growth and self-rediscovering in your daily routines for a sustainable and peaceful family, community, and environment.

For order and other details, please contact creativemindandthinkerbooks@gmail.com
Special discounts are also available.

Peace Is Love

PEACE IS LOVE.

Peace is loving everyone exceptionally. Children should keep loving and stop hating. Every parent, guardian, and teacher should try to educate their children about love. *Love* is the lubricant that smoothens the way toward a peaceful co-existence. As our world is facing a critical violence situation, its more reasons our children should learn about love, peace and not hate or discrimination.

PEACE ACCOMODATES

PEACE ACCOMMODATES.

A peaceful child treats everyone equally and accommodates every other child no matter the skin color, race, culture, or background. Peaceful children are the most precious pupils that our society needs, to transform our chaotic world into a lovely and peaceful haven.

PEACE APPRECIATES

PEACE APPRECIATES.

An act of appreciation is a moderate way of saying thank you or a sign of relief to the heart, especially when people do something good for you which includes your parents, granny, teachers, friends, and siblings. That is the same thing peace does; it appreciates good gestures, non-violent communication, good contributions, and never dismays; rather, it addresses, transforms, reverses, and encourages.

Where two or more peaceful, kind, and loving children are living, that community will keep smiling, and their lives will be better because there would not be any cause for alarm. All forms of radicalism will change with peace. Peace gives way for good ethical communication instead of confrontation, love in replacement of hate, tolerance in exchange for acrimony, mutual relationship for enmity, and respect for disrespect. Peace appreciates all forms of life, irrespective of culture, religion, race, tribe, and ethnicity.

PEACE IS BRAVE

PEACE IS BRAVE.

My child, you should endeavor and always seek peace and support a culture of peace. Children should understand that seeking peace does not make you a weakling. Self-defense technique is not bad, especially against tormentors, but a peaceful dialogue is far better than engaging in a fight.

Bravest children are known for their credibility and ability to transform or create. Peace is the only approach that knows how to save money, create jobs, reduce poverty and crisis, and ensure a non-conflicting atmosphere and that's why it's brave.

PEACE IS FUNDAMENTAL

PEACE IS FUNDAMENTAL.

Children, let peace become your daily process in life. Do you know why? Because children function more positively in a peaceful environment. They can ride their bicycles without any fear. They can walk alone in the park in peace without any fear of the unknown. Parents should teach their children to take peace as their primary priority in their respective home and community for a better peaceful and prospective world.

Peace is unbeatable, it has taken the best position in every sphere of life, and whatever money can buy, peace gives them freely without hassle. If you can discover the peace in you, be sure that you have the basic thing you need to conquer and overcome.

PEACE IS
GOLDEN

PEACE IS GOLDEN.

 Golden children are very peaceful, respectful, and intelligent. They are very exceptional and accommodating. However, do not hurt yourself while trying to please others because when you lose the peace in you, you would become empty. Always walk away from unfavorable, unhealthy, non-peaceful and unpleasant environments to protect your self-peace.

 As a golden child, you deserve a golden peace. Who`s a golden child? Every child is a precious asset to their parents and the whole universe.

PEACE
HEALS

PEACE HEALS.

Children, peace can heal our traumatic experiences and lonely hearts. We can become traumatized when betrayed, defamed, or lied against. In any condition you find yourself, always keep the peace in you and hold it firmly. Remember, there are rich people who are not happy because they lack peace within their inner selves and can only be better by true peace of mind.

Have you ever heard that peace heals the wounded heart? You might ask how. When the heart is sick, it needs only one thing – peace. When our life is in turmoil, it needs only peace to settle it. When we are in a state of devastation, peace is the solution. When we are weary and confused, peace is all we need. When we lose our loved ones, all we need is peace to keep us going.

PEACE IS
IMMACULATE

PEACE IS IMMACULATE.

My child, peace is purely immaculate and has no stain, the moment you can be at peace; you will see how bright and innocent your heart is. Your life will become better in such a way that whoever comes around you will appreciate you and can never be the same after that. Being immaculate stands for purity and an immaculate child comes from a peaceful home. Stop hating yourself because you are a precious and an innocent child.

PEACE IS JUSTICE

PEACE IS JUSTICE.

Children who stand for equal treatment and freedom are the future peace ambassadors. Do you want to be the most decorated peace ambassador in the future? Begin now to stand for peace, justice, equality, equity, and fairness.

Are you aware that children who seek justice would make good and incorruptible judges? Peace stands on justice for all for a better, free, and formidable world.

How does it achieve its goal? Peace brings the rich, poor, young, old, violent, and calm children together, engages them in dialogue, penalizes whoever does wrong through empathy, and then introduces peace into their system. Children should learn to transform our society with peace, love, tolerance, and understanding, which is unique to a better and joyful society.

PEACE IS MAGNETIC

PEACE IS MAGNETIC.

Children that have peace are very magnetic, attractive, and well loved. Because only their peaceful smile and empathetic nature can win them the most tremendous prize. When a parent, teacher or guardian can adequately train and enlighten a child about peace, the spirit of that child would be ready to attract by implication. Whatever its benefits, will magnetically attract good fortune regardless of distance or time.

PEACE IS PLEASANT

PEACE IS PLEASANT.

A pleasant child is noble and the greatest gift to their family, humanity, and society. A pleasant child is welcoming and always happy with people around them. Children as you like and cherish a variety of chocolate for distinct reasons, especially the great fun-filled taste and its color which is enticing and fascinating yet peace tastes much better and is more attractive and pleasant than chocolates. My child, let peace become your daily chocolate.

PEACE IS A RAINBOW

PEACE IS A RAINBOW.

The beauty of rainbows is a clear representation of peace which can work within us with an open heart. When children and adults see rainbows above the sky, we usually admire the splendid colors. My child, the moment we start appreciating peace, our hearts and outward dispositions will be to that of a beautiful rainbow above the sky. Children, peace is as beautiful as a rainbow above the sky.

Peace is the best gift ever that can transform our environment, community, and world. Only peace can stop the crisis in our world. A peaceful child will raise a peaceful family, which will produce a peaceful generation that will create a peaceful society/environment. This, in turn, will transform into a peaceful nation, and then a peaceful world will emerge.

PEACE REJUVENATES

PEACE REJUVENATES.

Children need to understand that having peace of mind always rejuvenates our sorrowful and awful state of mind. It can change our sadness and make us feel better. Children, always remember that when you are sad it is because you are unhappy and when you are not happy, there`s no peace in you.

When we are mentally or physically unstable with thoughts or worries, the peace in us and around us rejuvenates the weakened spirit, which helps it to keep moving. When we have lost our hope, peace energizes, empowers, and strengthens us. Peace is always the best approach.

PEACE IS SMART

PEACE IS SMART.

 Children function positively especially when they have peace of mind. Peace goes with empathy, love, passion, tolerance, perseverance, humility, and forgiveness. Peace taught us how to live longer and happier even without our parents having the best cars, houses, and jobs.

 Peace has made us understand that once we have peace in our lives, we are great.

PEACE IS WISE

PEACE IS WISE.

Children who have peace in their hearts are peaceful in nature. Wisdom is the best gift you could ever ask for, therefore wisest children understand that having peace is the only source that can help to remain focused because it brings happiness, harmony, smiles, energy, and love. Wisest children also know when to cry, laugh, study, work, and play.

AUTHOR`S NOTE.

Peace is being yourself, feeling good about yourself and helping others and your community.

The world is a better place because of you.

The rainbow I used in this book is the natural rainbow, therefore I am neither promoting nor kicking against any person`s choice of life.

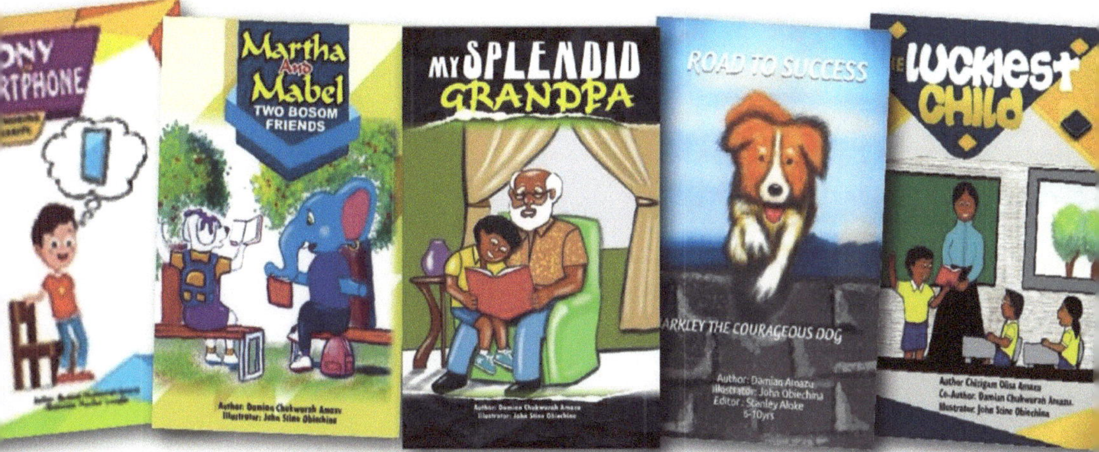

Our children's book collection
AVAILABLE ON AMAZON

Damian Chukwurah Amazu is an upcoming author of more than six books for children.

Other books by Damian Chukwurah Amazu

The Story of Sanga, The Tale of An African Child.

My Splendid Grandpa

Road To Success, Barkley the Courageous Dog.

Martha & Mabel, Two Bosom Friends.

The Irony of Smart Phone, the Diminishing of Humanity.

The Luckiest Child.

BRACE YOURSELF

What did you learn from the book?

1.

2.

3.

4.